Linda Doeser

bread

simple and delicious easy-to-make recipes
for your bread maker

This is a Parragon Book
This edition published in 2005

Parragon
Queen Street House
4 Queen Street
Bath BA1 1HE, UK

ISBN: 1-40546-225-6

Printed in China

Produced by
THE BRIDGEWATER BOOK COMPANY LTD

Photography Calvey Taylor-Haw
Home Economist Michaela Jester

Cover Photography Calvey Taylor-Haw
Home Economist Ruth Pollock

ALL THE RECIPES IN THIS BOOK ARE FOR USE WITH A BREAD MACHINE

- Always read the bread machine manufacturer's handbook. Although most bread machines work in basically the same way, there are some important variations from brand to brand.

- Add the ingredients in the order given in the ingredients list unless the instructions require you to add the dry ingredients first. In that case, simply reverse the order. Measure ingredients accurately. Do not mix the imperial and metric measures. All spoon measurements are level: teaspoons are assumed to be 5 ml and tablespoons are assumed to be 15 ml.

- Make sure that the kneading blade is properly attached. Do not plug the machine in until you are ready to switch it on. Always remove the bread pan to add the ingredients to avoid spills inside the machine.

- Ingredients should be at room temperature first. Use hand-hot liquid as this will activate the yeast. Make sure that flours and yeast are not past their 'use-by' dates.

- Do not open the bread machine during cooking, except when necessary for adding extra ingredients. Otherwise, the temperature will drop and the bread will be disappointing.

- Use oven gloves to remove the bread pan after baking – it will be very hot. Make sure the bread machine is on a level surface and cannot be reached by young children.

- Do not use the timer delay for recipes that include perishable ingredients, such as eggs, yogurt or buttermilk.

- The recipes in this book have been tested in medium-sized machines. They are all suitable for large machines and most will work successfully in small machines. Check the manufacturer's handbook for maximum capacity.

- For shaped loaves, follow the instructions for proving the dough (letting it rise). Place in a warm place, such as an airing cupboard. The dough may take longer to rise in a cooler place. Always preheat the oven fully before baking.

contents

introduction

There can be few more appetising aromas than the smell of bread baking and few more delicious tastes than a still-warm, freshly cooked loaf. With a bread machine, this can quickly become a trouble-free, everyday treat. If you have a timer delay, fresh bread every morning is even less trouble than brewing a pot of coffee.

The recipes in this book cover all kinds of bread for every occasion and lifestyle. There are simple, basic breads that require no more effort than measuring a few ingredients into the machine and pressing the start switch, yet even these provide a wide range of flavours, from a plain white loaf to a moist fruit bread.More ambitious cooks can use the machine to take the hard work out of making the dough, and create professional-looking plaits, baguettes, baps, breadsticks and Danish pastries. The versatility of the bread machine is further explored with mouthwatering pizza recipes, as well as some fabulous cakes to

poppy seed plait
page 14

orange marmalade loaf
page 40

perk up mid-morning coffee or afternoon tea.

Bread, in one form or another, features in the diets of every country in the world. The recipes in this book include a global round-up of French, Italian, Finnish, Indian, Hungarian, Austrian, Danish, Caribbean, Scottish and American specialities. It also includes some traditional English treats from different parts of the country, such as Cornish Saffron Bread and Devonshire Splits.

easy

Recipes are graded as follows:
1 spoon = easy;
2 spoons = very easy;
3 spoons = extremely easy.

1 small loaf

Recipes generally make a small or medium loaf, or the quantity is specified: e.g. two 25-cm/10-inch pizza bases.

15 minutes

Preparation time. Where marinating or soaking are involved, these times have been added on separately: eg, 15 minutes + 30 minutes to marinate.

40 minutes

Cooking time. Cooking times do not include the cooking of side dishes or accompaniments served with the main dishes.

fresh herb cottage loaf
page 58

sticky apricot & cinnamon buns
page 92

Here are some easy recipes for a wide range of different loaves. For the simplest, you just place all of the ingredients in the machine, press start, and turn out a perfect loaf to cool. Varying the ingredients produces a delicious selection of breads, from Wholemeal Harvest Bread to American Corn Bread. There are also popular breads and rolls for cooking in a conventional oven. Use the bread machine to make perfect dough, then turn out and shape. You will find that more specialist loaves, such as Poppy Seed Plait and French Baguettes, are well within the scope of the beginner.

family favourites

crusty white bread

extremely
easy

1 medium
loaf

10 minutes

about
3 hours

ingredients

1 egg

1 egg yolk

hand-hot water, as required

500 g/1 lb 2 oz strong white bread flour

1½ tsp salt

2 tsp sugar

25 g /1 oz butter, softened or diced

1 tsp easy-blend dried yeast

Put the egg and egg yolk into a measuring jug and beat lightly to mix. Add sufficient hand-hot water to make up to 300 ml/10 fl oz. Stir to mix then pour into the bread pan.

Sprinkle the flour over the liquid to cover. Place the salt, sugar and butter in 3 corners of the pan. Indent the flour without exposing the liquid and add the yeast.

Set the bread machine to the basic setting, medium crust, and press start.

When the cycle has finished, turn out the bread to cool.

wholemeal harvest bread

extremely easy   1 small loaf

5 minutes   about 3½ hours

ingredients

175 ml/6 fl oz hand-hot water
1½ tbsp sunflower oil
225 g/8 oz strong wholemeal bread flour
1 tbsp skimmed milk powder

1 tsp salt
2 tbsp soft brown sugar
1 tsp easy-blend dried yeast

Pour the water into the bread pan and add the sunflower oil.

Sprinkle the flour over the liquid to cover, then sprinkle in the skimmed milk powder. Place the salt and sugar in 2 corners of the pan. Indent the flour without exposing the liquid and add the yeast.

Set the bread machine to the wholemeal setting, medium crust, and press start.

When the cycle has finished, turn out the bread to cool.

milk loaf

extremely easy

1 medium loaf

5 minutes

about 3 hours

ingredients

200 ml/7 fl oz hand-hot full cream
  or semi-skimmed milk
100 ml/3½ fl oz hand-hot water
450 g/1 lb strong white bread flour

1½ tsp salt
2 tsp sugar
25 g/1 oz butter, softened or diced
1 tsp easy-blend dried yeast

Pour the milk and water into the bread pan.

Sprinkle the flour over the liquid to cover. Place the salt, sugar and butter in 3 corners of the pan. Indent the flour without exposing the liquid and add the yeast.

Set the bread machine to the basic setting, medium crust, and press start.

When the cycle has finished, turn out the bread to cool.

poppy seed plait

easy   1 loaf

2¼ hours   30–35 minutes

ingredients

175 ml/6 fl oz hand-hot water

2 tbsp sunflower oil, plus extra
  for greasing

225 g/8 oz strong white bread flour, plus
  extra for dusting

2 tbsp skimmed milk powder

1 tsp salt

1½ tbsp sugar

1 tsp easy-blend dried yeast

3 tbsp poppy seeds

TOPPING

1 egg yolk

1 tbsp milk

1 tbsp caster sugar

2 tbsp poppy seeds

Pour the water into the bread pan and add the sunflower oil. Sprinkle the flour over the liquid to cover, then add the skimmed milk powder. Place the salt and sugar in 2 corners of the pan. Indent the flour without exposing the liquid and add the yeast.

Set the bread machine to the dough setting and press start. Five minutes before the end, add the poppy seeds. Remove the finished dough from the pan. Knock back gently on a floured surface and knead lightly. Divide into 3 equal pieces and shape each piece into a rope. Plait the ropes, pinch them together at each end and tuck under. Place on an oiled baking sheet, cover with clingfilm, and set aside in a warm place to rise for 30 minutes.

For the topping, lightly beat the egg yolk with the milk and sugar. Remove the clingfilm and brush over the loaf, then sprinkle over the poppy seeds. Bake in a preheated oven, 200°C/400°F/Gas Mark 6, for 30–35 minutes, until golden. Turn out the bread to cool.

french baguettes

easy   2 loaves

4 hours   15–20
minutes

325 ml/11 fl oz hand-hot water
450 g/1 lb strong white bread flour,
  plus extra for dusting

1½ tsp salt
1½ tsp easy-blend dried yeast
sunflower oil, for greasing

Pour the water into the bread pan. Sprinkle the flour over the liquid to cover. Place the salt in a corner of the pan. Indent the flour without exposing the liquid and add the yeast. Set the machine to French dough setting and press start.

Remove the finished dough from the pan. Knock back on a lightly floured surface, then divide in half. Shape each piece into a ball then roll out into 2 rectangles. With the long sides facing, fold the top third of each rectangle down and the bottom third up and press together. Repeat twice more with each rectangle, resting the dough in between each folding. Gently roll and stretch each piece of dough, in turn, into a stick about 30 cm/12 inches long.

Place between the folds of a pleated tea towel for support and cover with oiled clingfilm. Set aside in a warm place for 30–40 minutes to rise. Remove the clingfilm. Slash the tops diagonally. Dampen the inside of a preheated oven, 230°C/450°F/Gas Mark 8. Bake for 15–20 minutes.

potato & oatmeal bread

very easy   1 medium loaf

40 minutes   about 3 hours

ingredients

225 g/8 oz floury potatoes (peeled weight)
210 ml/7½ fl oz hand-hot water
500 g/1 lb 2 oz strong white bread flour
3 tbsp rolled oats
2 tbsp skimmed milk powder
1½ tsp salt
1½ tbsp dark brown sugar
40 g/1½ oz butter, softened or diced
1½ tsp easy-blend dried yeast

TOPPING
1 tbsp water
1 tbsp rolled oats

Place the potatoes in a pan, add water to cover, bring to the boil and cook for 20–25 minutes, until tender. Drain and mash until smooth. Set aside to cool.

Pour the water into the bread pan. Sprinkle the flour over the liquid to cover, then sprinkle in the rolled oats and skimmed milk powder. Add the mashed potatoes to the bread pan, then place the salt, sugar and butter in 3 corners of the pan. Indent the flour without exposing the liquid and add the yeast.

Set the bread machine to the basic setting, medium crust, and press start. About 5 minutes before the end of the final rising cycle (about 1¼ hours from the start), add the topping. Brush the top of the loaf with the water and carefully sprinkle over the rolled oats.

When the cycle has finished, turn out the bread to cool.

pitta breads

very easy   6 pittas

2 hours   5 minutes

ingredients

210 ml/7½ fl oz hand-hot water
350 g/12 oz strong white bread flour,
   plus extra for dusting
1½ tsp salt

1 tsp sugar
1 tsp easy-blend dried yeast
1 tbsp olive oil, plus extra for greasing

Pour the water into the bread pan. Sprinkle the flour over the liquid to cover. Place the salt and sugar in 2 corners of the pan. Indent the flour without exposing the liquid. Add the yeast and the oil. Set the bread machine to the pizza dough setting and press start.

Remove the finished dough from the bread pan. Knock back gently on a lightly floured surface, then divide into 6 equal pieces. Shape each piece into a ball and place on a tray. Cover with oiled clingfilm and set aside for 10 minutes. Meanwhile, place 2–3 baking sheets in the oven and preheat to 230°C/450°F/Gas Mark 8.

Uncover the dough and flatten each piece slightly. Roll out each piece into a round. Sprinkle lightly with flour and cover with oiled clingfilm. Set aside for 10 minutes to rest. Remove the clingfilm and transfer the rounds to the baking sheets, spaced well apart. Bake for 5 minutes, until risen and golden. Turn out to cool.

american corn bread

extremely easy

1 small loaf

5 minutes

about 1¾ hours

ingredients

150 ml/5 fl oz hand-hot water

5 tbsp hand-hot milk

1 tbsp corn oil

280 g/10 oz strong white bread flour

100 g/3½ oz fine cornmeal

1 tsp salt

1½ tsp light brown sugar

1 tsp easy-blend dried yeast

TOPPING

1 tbsp water

1 tbsp medium cornmeal

Pour the water, milk and corn oil into the bread pan.

Sprinkle the flour over the liquid to cover, then sprinkle in the fine cornmeal. Place the salt and sugar in 2 corners of the pan. Indent the flour without exposing the liquid and add the yeast.

Set the bread machine to the quick setting, medium crust, and press start. About 5 minutes before baking begins (about 20 minutes from the start) add the topping. Brush the top of the dough with the water and carefully sprinkle with the medium cornmeal.

When the cycle has finished, turn out the bread to cool.

floury baps

very easy 10 baps

2¼ hours 15–20
minutes

ingredients

140 ml/4½ fl oz hand-hot water
140 ml/4½ fl oz hand-hot milk
450 g/1 lb strong white bread flour,
  plus extra for dusting
1½ tsp salt

2 tsp caster sugar
1 tsp easy-blend dried yeast
sunflower oil, for greasing
milk, for glazing

Pour the water and milk into the bread pan. Sprinkle the flour over the liquid to cover. Place the salt and sugar in 2 corners of the pan. Indent the flour without exposing the liquid and add the yeast. Set the bread machine to the dough setting and press start.

Remove the finished dough from the pan. Knock back gently on a lightly floured surface. Divide it into 10 equal pieces. Place on a tray and cover with lightly oiled clingfilm. Uncover one by one and shape into balls, then roll out into 10-cm/4-inch-long ovals. Cover with lightly oiled clingfilm and set aside in a warm place for about 30 minutes to rise. Remove the clingfilm and gently press the centre of each bap to release any large air bubbles.

Brush the tops with milk and dust with flour. Bake on 2 oiled baking sheets in a preheated oven, 200°C/400°F/Gas Mark 6, for 15–20 minutes, until lightly browned. Cool slightly. Serve warm.

sesame breadsticks

very easy

30 breadsticks

2¼ hours

15–20 minutes

ingredients

200 ml/7 fl oz hand-hot water
3 tbsp olive oil, plus extra for greasing
   and brushing
350 g/12 oz strong white bread flour,
   plus extra for dusting

1½ tsp salt
1½ tsp easy-blend dried yeast
sesame seeds, for coating

Pour the water into the bread pan and add the olive oil. Sprinkle the flour over the liquid to cover. Place the salt in 1 corner. Indent the flour without exposing the liquid and add the yeast. Set the bread machine to the dough setting and press start.

Remove the finished dough from the pan. Knock back on a lightly floured surface and roll out into a 23 x 20-cm/9 x 8-inch rectangle. Cut the dough into 3 strips, each 20 cm/8 inches long, then cut each strip across into 10 equal pieces. Gently roll and stretch each piece into a stick about 30 cm/12 inches long. Roll in the sesame seeds to coat, then place on oiled baking sheets. Brush with oil, cover with clingfilm and set aside in a warm place for 15 minutes. Remove the clingfilm and bake the breadsticks in a preheated oven, 200°C/400°F/Gas Mark 6, for 10 minutes. Turn them over, return to the oven and bake for a further 5–10 minutes, until golden. Turn out the breadsticks to cool.

Life today is so rushed that most of us barely have time to grab a slice of toast in the morning. These recipes are designed to provide an energy boost to get you going. They are as packed with flavour as they are with nutritional goodness. What could make a better start to the day than Orange Marmalade Loaf, unless it is Muesli Bread? The recipes also include some truly luxurious morning treats for weekends, holidays and special occasions. Impress overnight guests with home-made Petits Pains aux Chocolat, or serve freshly griddled English Muffins for brunch.

breakfast bakes

muesli bread

very easy | 1 medium loaf

2¾–3 hours | 30–35 minutes

ingredients

250 ml/8 fl oz hand-hot water

2 tbsp sunflower oil, plus extra for greasing

1 tbsp clear honey

300 g/10½ oz strong white bread flour

85 g/3 oz wholemeal bread flour, plus extra for dusting

150 g/5½ oz unsweetened muesli

3 tbsp skimmed milk powder

1½ tsp salt

1½ tsp easy-blend dried yeast

70 g/2½ oz ready-to-eat dried apricots, chopped

Put the water, sunflower oil and honey into the bread pan.

Sprinkle both types of flour over the liquid to cover, then sprinkle in the muesli and skimmed milk powder. Place the salt in 1 corner of the pan. Indent the flour without exposing the liquid and add the yeast.

Set the bread machine to the dough setting and press start. Five minutes before the end of kneading, add the dried apricots.

Remove the finished dough from the pan. Knock back gently on a lightly floured surface, then shape into a round. Place the loaf on a lightly oiled baking sheet. Cut a deep cross in the top with a sharp knife. Cover with lightly oiled clingfilm and set aside in a warm place for about 30–40 minutes to rise. Remove the clingfilm and bake the loaf in a preheated oven, 200°C/400°F/Gas Mark 6, for 30–35 minutes, until golden. Turn out the bread to cool.

banana & orange bread

ingredients

very easy 1 medium
loaf

5 minutes about
3 hours

4 tbsp orange juice
200 ml/7 fl oz hand-hot buttermilk
  or water
2 medium ripe bananas or 1 large ripe
  banana, peeled and mashed
3 tbsp clear honey
500 g/1 lb 2 oz strong white bread flour,
  plus an extra 1–2 tbsp for sticky dough

1½ tbsp skimmed milk powder, optional
1 tsp salt
40 g/1½ oz butter, softened or diced
1 tsp easy-blend dried yeast
milk, for glazing, optional

Pour the orange juice and buttermilk into the bread pan.

Add the mashed bananas and honey. Sprinkle the flour over the liquid and fruit
to cover. If using water, sprinkle the skimmed milk powder over the flour (it is not
necessary if you have used buttermilk). Place the salt and butter in 2 corners of
the bread pan. Indent the flour without exposing the liquid and add the yeast.

Set the bread machine to the basic setting, medium crust, and press start. If
the dough looks very sticky towards the end of the first kneading, add a further
1–2 tablespoons of strong white bread flour. (The stickiness depends on the
ripeness and size of the bananas.)

Just before the baking cycle starts (about 2 hours after the start), brush the top
of the loaf with milk to glaze, if desired. When the cycle has finished, turn out the
bread to cool.

bran & yogurt bread

extremely easy 1 small loaf

5 minutes about 3 hours

ingredients

150 ml/5 fl oz hand-hot water

125 ml/4 fl oz natural yogurt, at room temperature

1 tbsp sunflower oil

1 tbsp treacle or golden syrup

200 g/7 oz strong white bread flour

150 g/5½ oz strong wholemeal bread flour

25 g/1 oz wheat bran

1 tsp salt

¾ tsp easy-blend dried yeast

Pour the water into the bread pan and add the yogurt, sunflower oil and treacle.

Sprinkle both types of flour over the liquid to cover. Place the wheat bran and salt in 2 corners of the pan. Indent the flour without exposing the liquid and add the yeast.

Set the bread machine to the basic setting, medium crust, and press start.

When the cycle has finished, turn out the bread to cool.

mixed seed bread

extremely easy   1 medium loaf

5 minutes   about 3 hours

ingredients

300 ml/10 fl oz hand-hot water
1½ tbsp sunflower oil
2 tsp lemon juice
375 g/13 oz strong white bread flour
125 g/4½ oz rye flour
1½ tbsp skimmed milk powder
1½ tsp salt
1 tbsp light brown sugar
1 tsp caraway seeds

½ tsp poppy seeds
½ tsp sesame seeds
1 tsp easy-blend dried yeast

TOPPING
1 egg white
1 tbsp water
1 tbsp sunflower or pumpkin seeds

Pour the water into the bread pan and add the sunflower oil and lemon juice. Sprinkle both the flours over the liquid to cover, then sprinkle in the skimmed milk powder. Place the salt, sugar and seeds in 3 corners of the pan. Indent the flour without exposing the liquid and add the yeast.

Set the bread machine to the basic setting, medium crust, and press start.

For the topping, lightly beat the egg white with the water to make a glaze. Just before the baking cycle starts (about 2 hours after the start), brush the glaze over the loaf, then gently press the sunflower or pumpkin seeds all over the top.

When the cycle has finished, turn out the bread to cool.

spicy cinnamon bread

very easy   1 small loaf

25 minutes   about
             3 hours

ingredients

350 g/12 oz plain flour
1½ tsp baking powder
¼ tsp salt
1 tsp ground cinnamon
½ tsp mixed spice
½ tsp freshly grated nutmeg
½ tsp ground ginger

55 g/2 oz butter
4 tbsp treacle
3 eggs, beaten lightly
50 ml/2 fl oz milk
25 g/1 oz raisins
55 g/2 oz dried apple rings,
    snipped into pieces

Sift the flour, baking powder, salt and spices into a mixing bowl and set aside.

Put the butter and treacle into a saucepan over a low heat, stirring constantly, until the butter has melted. Leave to cool slightly, then stir in the eggs, milk, raisins and apple pieces. Add the treacle mixture to the flour mixture and stir gently until combined.

Turn the mixture into the bread pan. Set the bread machine to the cake setting and press start.

When the cycle has finished, turn out the bread to cool.

orange marmalade loaf

easy   1 medium loaf

2¾ hours   25–30 minutes

ingredients

150 ml/5 fl oz hand-hot water

150 ml/5 fl oz hand-hot milk

2 tbsp sunflower oil, plus extra
for greasing

450 g/1 lb strong white bread flour,
plus extra for dusting

1½ tsp salt

1½ tsp sugar

1½ tsp easy-blend dried yeast

7 tbsp orange marmalade

TOPPING

1 egg yolk

1 tbsp milk

1 tbsp caster sugar

1–2 tbsp crystallised orange peel

Pour the water and milk into the bread pan and add the oil. Sprinkle the flour over the liquid to cover. Put the salt and sugar in 2 corners. Indent the flour without exposing the liquid and add the yeast. Set the bread machine to the dough setting and press start.

Remove the dough from the bread pan. Knock back gently on a lightly floured surface. Roll out to a rectangle about 2 cm/¾ inch thick. Spread over the marmalade, leaving a 1-cm/½-inch border on one long side. Roll up like as Swiss roll and place seam-side down in a greased loaf tin. Cover with lightly oiled clingfilm and set aside in a warm place for about 45 minutes to rise. Remove the clingfilm.

For the topping, lightly beat the egg yolk, milk and sugar. Brush over the loaf. Score the top and arrange the orange peel over it. Bake in a preheated oven, 220°C/425°F/Gas Mark 7, for 25–30 minutes, until golden. Turn out the bread to cool.

brioche

easy   1 loaf

3 hours   40–45 minutes

ingredients

2 eggs, at room temperature
2 tbsp hand-hot milk
225 g/8 oz strong white bread flour, plus
   extra for dusting
½ tsp salt
1 tbsp caster sugar
55 g/2 oz butter, melted
1½ tsp easy-blend dried yeast
sunflower oil, for greasing

GLAZE
1 egg yolk
1 tbsp milk or water

Lightly beat the eggs with the milk in a bowl, then pour into the bread pan. Sprinkle the flour over the liquid to cover. Place the salt, sugar and butter in 3 corners of the pan. Indent the flour without exposing the liquid and add the yeast. Set the bread machine to the dough setting and press start. With the lid shut, let the dough rise in the machine for an extra 30 minutes.

Remove the finished dough from the pan. Knock back gently on a floured surface. Slice off a quarter, wrap in oiled clingfilm and set aside. Oil a brioche mould. Knead the large piece of dough, shape into a ball, and place in the mould and indent the top. Unwrap the smaller piece and lightly knead into a pear shape. Place on top. Cover with clingfilm and set aside in a warm place for about 1 hour to rise. Remove the clingfilm. For the glaze, lightly beat the egg yolk with the milk. Brush over the top. Bake in a preheated oven, 220°C/425°F/Gas Mark 7, for 40–45 minutes, until golden.

english muffins

very easy   10–11
             muffins

2 hours   35–40
             minutes

ingredients

350 ml/12 fl oz hand-hot milk
450 g/1 lb strong white bread flour, or
   225 g/8 oz strong white bread flour plus
   225 g/8 oz strong wholemeal bread flour,
   plus extra for dusting
1½ tsp salt

1 tsp caster sugar
15 g/½ oz butter, softened or diced
1½ tsp easy-blend dried yeast
ground rice or rice flour, for dusting
sunflower oil, for greasing

Pour the milk into the bread pan. Sprinkle the flour over the liquid to cover.
Place the salt, sugar and butter in 3 corners of the pan. Indent the flour without
exposing the liquid and add the yeast. Set the bread machine to the dough setting
and press start.

Remove the finished dough from the bread pan. Knock back gently on a lightly
floured surface, then roll out to 1 cm/½ inch thick. Stamp out rounds with a
7.5-cm/3-inch plain pastry cutter. Gather up the trimmings, knead together
and leave to rest for 3–4 minutes. Re-roll and stamp out another 1–2 muffins.

Place the muffins on a dusted baking sheet. Dust the tops with ground rice.
Cover with oiled clingfilm and set aside in a warm place for 20–25 minutes to rise.
Remove the clingfilm. Lightly oil a griddle pan or heavy frying pan and heat well.
Cook the muffins in batches, over a low heat, for 6–7 minutes on each side.
Serve warm.

petits pains aux chocolat

easy

9 petits pains

about 4 hours

15 minutes

ingredients

125 ml/4 fl oz hand-hot water
250 g/9 oz strong white bread flour
2 tbsp skimmed milk powder
½ tsp salt
1 tbsp caster sugar
140 g/5 oz butter, softened,
  plus extra for greasing
1½ tsp easy-blend dried yeast

sunflower oil, for greasing
225 g/8 oz plain chocolate,
  broken into pieces

GLAZE
1 egg yolk, beaten
1 tsp milk

Pour the water into the bread pan. Sprinkle in the flour and milk powder. Add the salt, sugar and 25 g/1 oz of the butter in 3 corners of the pan. Indent the flour then add the yeast. Set the machine at dough setting and press start. Shape the remaining butter into a rectangle 2 cm /¾ inch thick. Knock back the finished dough, shape into a ball and cut a cross in the centre. Roll out the edges around the cross. Place the butter in the centre and seal the edges over it. Roll out into a rectangle. With one short side towards you, fold the bottom-third up and the top-third down and seal. Wrap in clingfilm. Chill for 20 minutes. Repeat twice more, finally chilling for 30 minutes.

Roll out the dough into a large rectangle. Cut into 9 even pieces. Place chocolate pieces on each at a short end. Combine the egg yolk and milk, and brush over the edges. Roll up and seal. Place on oiled baking trays, seam-side down. Wrap and set aside for 30 minutes to rise. Brush with the remaining glaze. Bake in a preheated oven, 200°C/400°F/Gas Mark 6, for 15 minutes.

flaky almond pastries

easy   12 pastries

3½–4 hours   15 minutes

ingredients

DANISH PASTRY

5 tbsp hand-hot milk

2 eggs, one separated

225 g/8 oz strong white bread flour,
   plus extra for dusting

½ tsp salt

1 tbsp caster sugar

140 g/5 oz butter, softened

½ tsp easy-blend dried yeast

sunflower oil, for greasing

1 tbsp water

flaked almonds, for sprinkling

FILLING

1 tbsp butter

85 g/3 oz caster sugar

85 g/3 oz ground almonds

2–3 drops almond essence

1 small egg, beaten lightly

For the pastry, pour the milk into the bread pan and add one egg. Add the flour, salt, sugar and 25 g/1 oz of the butter. Indent the mixture and add yeast. Set the bread machine at dough setting. Press start. Shape the remaining butter into a 2-cm/¾-inch-thick rectangle. Roll the finished dough into a rectangle. Place the butter on one half, fold the other half over and seal. Roll out again into a rectangle. With one short side towards you, fold the top-third down and the bottom-third up, then seal. Wrap in clingfilm and chill for 15 minutes. Repeat twice more. Finally wrap and chill for 20 minutes.

For the filling, cream the butter and sugar. Add the almonds and essence. Mix to a paste with the beaten egg. Roll out the dough. Cut into 12 squares. Spread filling on half of each square. Brush the pastry edges with the white from the separated egg, fold over, and seal. Set aside on a greased baking sheet for 30 minutes to rise. Beat the egg yolk and water and glaze the pastries. Add the almonds. Bake in a preheated oven, 200°C/400°F/Gas Mark 6, for 15 minutes.

These substantial and flavour-packed loaves are ideal for turning a snack into a satisfying and nourishing lunch. They also add the perfect touch to a family supper or an informal dinner party. Herbs, spices, cheese and nuts can all be easily incorporated into the dough to create a loaf that will really liven up a meal. Impress your guests by choosing from international favourites to match your main course. If you are serving a curry, why not make some Coriander and Garlic Naan? And what could go better with pasta than Sun-dried Tomato and Basil Ciabatta?

savoury breads

rosemary bread

extremely easy

1 medium loaf

10 minutes

about 3 hours

ingredients

160 ml/5½ fl oz hand-hot water

2 eggs, beaten lightly

4 tbsp olive oil

500g/1 lb 2 oz strong white bread flour

2 tbsp skimmed milk powder

1 tbsp finely chopped fresh rosemary

1½ tsp salt

2 tsp sugar

1 tsp easy-blend dried yeast

115 g/4 oz dried figs, chopped roughly

Pour the water into the bread pan and add the eggs and olive oil.

Sprinkle the flour over the liquid to cover, then sprinkle in the skimmed milk powder and the rosemary. Place the salt and sugar in 2 corners of the pan. Indent the flour without exposing the liquid and add the yeast.

Set the bread machine to the basic setting, medium crust, and press start. Five minutes before the end of kneading, add the figs.

When the cycle has finished, turn out the bread to cool.

greek olive & feta bread

very easy   1 medium loaf

2½ hours   35–40 minutes

ingredients

210 ml/7½ fl oz hand-hot water
375 g/13 oz strong white bread flour,
   plus extra for dusting
1 tbsp skimmed milk powder
1 tsp salt
1½ tsp sugar

1 tsp easy-blend dried yeast
55 g/2 oz stoned black olives, chopped
55 g/2 oz feta cheese, crumbled
olive oil, for brushing and greasing
herbs for sprinkling

Pour the water into the bread pan. Sprinkle the flour over the liquid to cover, then sprinkle in the skimmed milk powder. Place the salt and sugar in 2 corners of the pan. Indent the flour without exposing the liquid and add the yeast.

Set the bread machine to the dough setting. Five minutes before the end of kneading, add the olives and feta.

Remove the finished dough from the bread pan. Gently knock back the dough on a lightly floured surface. Shape the dough into a round loaf 20 cm/8 inches in diameter. Place it in an oiled 20-cm/8-inch-diameter round cake tin, cover with oiled clingfilm and set aside in a warm place for 40–45 minutes to rise.

Remove the clingfilm and brush the top of the loaf with olive oil and sprinkle with herbs. Bake in a preheated oven, 200°C/400°F/Gas Mark 6, for 35–40 minutes, until golden. Turn out the bread to cool.

fresh herb cottage loaf

very easy

1 loaf

2½ hours

30–35 minutes

ingredients

300 ml/10 fl oz hand-hot water

450 g/1 lb strong white bread flour, plus extra for dusting

1½ tsp salt

1½ tsp sugar

1½ tsp easy-blend dried yeast

2 tbsp chopped fresh parsley

2 tbsp chopped fresh chives

1 tbsp chopped fresh thyme

sunflower oil, for greasing

GLAZE

1 tbsp water

1 tbsp salt

Pour the water into the bread pan. Sprinkle the flour over the liquid to cover. Place the salt and sugar in 2 corners of the pan. Indent the flour without exposing the liquid and add the yeast. Set the bread machine to the dough setting. Five minutes before the end of kneading, add all the herbs.

Remove the finished dough from the pan. Knock back on a gently floured surface, then cut off one-third of the dough. Shape each piece into a ball. Cover with oiled clingfilm and set aside in a warm place for 30 minutes to rise. Unwrap the dough and cut a cross in the top of the larger piece. Brush with water and place the smaller piece on top. Make a hole through the centre of both balls of dough. Cover and set aside in a warm place for 10 minutes to rise.

Mix the water and salt and glaze the loaf. Slash around the loaf and dust with flour. Bake in a preheated oven, 220°C/425°F/Gas Mark 7, for 30–35 minutes, until golden. Turn out to cool.

finnish rye & caraway bread

extremely easy

1 medium loaf

10 minutes

about 3½ hours

ingredients

350 ml/12 fl oz hand-hot water

2 tbsp sunflower oil

2½ tbsp treacle

250 g/9 oz strong white bread flour

140 g/5 oz rye flour

85 g/3 oz wholemeal flour

75 g/2¾ oz dried breadcrumbs

3 tbsp oat bran

1½ tsp salt

1½ tbsp cocoa powder

2 tsp caraway seeds

½ tsp easy-blend dried yeast

Pour the water into the bread pan and add the oil and treacle.

Sprinkle all 3 types of flour over the liquid to cover, then sprinkle in the breadcrumbs and bran. Place the salt, cocoa powder and caraway seeds in 3 corners of the pan. Indent the flour without exposing the liquid and add the yeast.

Set the bread machine to the wholemeal setting, medium crust, and press start.

When the cycle has finished, turn out the bread to cool.

sun-dried tomato & basil ciabatta

easy   2 loaves

14 hours   25–30 minutes

ingredients

ITALIAN SPONGE
200 ml/7 fl oz hand-hot water
175 g/6 oz strong white bread flour
½ tsp easy-blend dried yeast

DOUGH
200 ml/7 fl oz hand-hot water
2 tbsp olive oil, plus extra for greasing
2 tbsp milk

325 g/11½ oz strong white bread flour, plus
   extra for dusting
1½ tsp salt
½ tsp sugar
¼ tsp easy-blend dried yeast
40 g/1½ oz drained sun-dried tomatoes in
   oil, chopped roughly, additional for
   topping if required
2 tbsp shredded fresh basil

For the sponge, pour the water into the bread pan. Sprinkle the flour over the liquid to cover. Indent the flour without exposing the liquid and add the yeast. Set the bread machine to the dough setting and press start. After 5 minutes, switch off the machine and leave for 12 hours. For the dough, pour the water into the bread pan with the Italian sponge. Add the oil and milk. Sprinkle the flour over the liquid to cover. Place the salt and sugar in 2 corners of the pan. Indent the flour without exposing the liquid and add the yeast. Set the machine to the dough setting. Five minutes before the end of kneading, add the sun-dried tomatoes and basil.

Transfer the finished dough to a bowl, cover with clingfilm and set aside in a warm place for about 1 hour to rise. Turn out and shape into two rectangular loaves about 2.5 cm/1 inch thick. Dust with flour and set aside, uncovered, in a warm place for 30 minutes to rise. Add a topping if required. Bake on oiled baking sheets in a preheated oven, 220°C/425°F/Gas Mark 7, for 25–30 minutes, until golden.

coriander & garlic naan

easy   3 flatbreads

1¾ hours   6–8 minutes

ingredients

100 ml/3½ fl oz hand-hot water
4 tbsp natural yogurt
280 g/10 oz strong white bread flour
1 garlic clove, chopped finely
1 tsp ground coriander
1 tsp salt
2 tsp clear honey

1 tbsp ghee or butter, melted,
 plus extra for brushing
1 tsp easy-blend dried yeast
sunflower oil, for greasing
1 tsp black onion seeds
1 tbsp chopped fresh coriander

Pour the water into the bread pan and add the yogurt. Sprinkle the flour over the liquid to cover, then sprinkle in the garlic and ground coriander. Place the salt, honey and melted ghee in 3 corners of the pan. Indent the flour without exposing the liquid and add the yeast. Set the bread machine to the dough setting or pizza dough setting and press start.

Place 3 baking sheets in the oven to preheat to 240°C/475°F/Gas Mark 9. Remove the finished dough from the bread pan. Knock back on a lightly floured surface and divide into 3 pieces. Shape each piece into a ball and cover 2 of them with oiled clingfilm. Roll the uncovered piece into a teardrop shape about 8 mm//³⁄₈ inch thick. Cover with oiled clingfilm, then roll out the other pieces of dough in turn. Remove the clingfilm and place on hot baking sheets and sprinkle with the onion seeds and chopped coriander. Bake for about 5 minutes, until puffed up. Grill and brush with melted ghee and serve warm.

Home-made pizza is a special treat and, with a bread machine, making perfect pizza dough is simplicity itself. This chapter includes recipes for different kinds of dough. It's up to you whether you make thin-crust or thick-crust, large or individual pizzas – there is also a recipe for calzone, a sort of inside-out pizza. The recipes here include a selection of toppings, but you can substitute your favourite ingredients for tailor-made pizzas to suit all the family. This chapter also provides recipes for focaccia and the Provençal recipe, Pissaladière.

light lunches
& suppers

pepperoni & red onion pizza

easy

2 x 25-cm/
10-inch pizzas

about
2 hours

20–30
minutes

ingredients

DOUGH

225 ml/7½ fl oz hand-hot water

15 g/½ oz butter, melted

325 g/11½ oz strong white bread flour, plus
  extra for dusting

1 tsp salt

2 tbsp sugar

1 tsp easy-blend dried yeast

olive oil, for greasing

TOPPING

4 tbsp sun-dried tomato paste

4 tomatoes, skinned and sliced thinly

2 red onions, chopped finely

4 slices prosciutto, shredded

12 slices pepperoni sausage

12 black olives

salt

¾ tsp herbes de Provence

55 g/2 oz mozzarella cheese, grated

olive oil, for drizzling

Pour the water into the bread pan and add the melted butter. Sprinkle the flour over the liquid to cover. Place the salt and sugar in 2 corners of the pan. Indent the flour without exposing the liquid and add the yeast. Set the bread machine to the pizza dough or dough setting and press start.

Remove the finished dough from the pan. Knock back gently on a lightly floured surface and divide in half. Roll out each piece of dough into a 25-cm/10-inch round and place on greased pizza pans or baking sheets. Push up the edges slightly. Cover with lightly oiled clingfilm and set aside to rest for 15 minutes.

For the topping, spread the sun-dried tomato paste evenly over each round. Arrange the tomato slices on top. Sprinkle over the onion, prosciutto, pepperoni and olives. Add the seasoning, herbs and grated cheese and drizzle with olive oil. Bake in a preheated oven, 220°C/425°F/Gas Mark 7, for 20–30 minutes, until sizzling.

chargrilled vegetable calzone

easy   2 calzones

about   20–30
2½ hours   minutes

ingredients

DOUGH
140 ml/4½ fl oz hand-hot water
2 tbsp olive oil, plus extra for greasing
  and brushing
225 g/8 oz strong white bread flour
1 tsp salt
½ tsp sugar
1 tsp easy-blend dried yeast

FILLING
1 red onion, cut into wedges
2 garlic cloves, skin left on

2 baby aubergines, quartered lengthways
2 courgettes, halved lengthways
1 small red pepper, deseeded and quartered
  lengthways
1 small orange pepper, deseeded and
  quartered lengthways
4 tbsp olive oil
1 tbsp balsamic vinegar
1 tbsp chopped fresh parsley
salt and pepper
85 g/3 oz goat's cheese, diced

Pour the water into the bread pan and add the olive oil. Sprinkle the flour over
the liquid to cover. Add the salt and sugar. Indent the flour without exposing the
liquid and add the yeast. Set the machine to the pizza dough or dough setting
and press start. Remove the dough from the pan. Knock back gently on a lightly
floured surface and divide in half. Roll out each piece into a round about
5 mm/¼ inch thick and place on a baking sheet. Cover with lightly oiled
clingfilm and set aside to rest for 15 minutes.

Place the vegetables in a roasting tin. Combine the oil, vinegar, parsley
and seasoning and pour over the top. Roast for about 15 minutes, at
200°C/400°F/Gas Mark 6, turning once. Cool. Peel off the garlic and pepper
skins and cover half of each dough round with vegetables and the goat's cheese,
leaving a border. Brush the edges with water and fold the halves over and seal.
Brush with olive oil and bake in a preheated oven, 220°C/425°F/Gas Mark 7,
for 20–30 minutes, until golden.

mozzarella & rosemary focaccia

ingredients

easy   1 loaf

2¼ hours   20–25
          minutes

210 ml/7½ fl oz hand-hot water
1 tbsp olive oil, plus extra for greasing
350 g/12 oz strong white bread flour,
   plus extra for dusting
½ tsp salt
1 tsp sugar
1 tsp easy-blend dried yeast
140 g/5 oz mozzarella cheese, grated

TOPPING
2 tbsp olive oil
fresh rosemary sprigs
coarse sea salt

Pour the water into the bread pan and add the oil. Sprinkle the flour over the liquid to cover. Place the salt and sugar in 2 corners of the pan. Indent the flour without exposing the liquid and add the yeast. Set the bread machine to the pizza dough or dough setting and press start.

Remove the finished dough from the pan. Knock back and gently flatten on a floured surface. Sprinkle over the mozzarella and knead. Shape into a ball, flatten slightly, then roll out into a 25-cm/10-inch round. Place in a lightly oiled cake tin. Cover with lightly oiled clingfilm and set aside in a warm place for 20 minutes to rise. Remove the clingfilm. Make indentations in the surface of the dough. Cover again and set aside in a warm place to rise for 15 minutes. Remove the clingfilm. Drizzle over the olive oil, then sprinkle with the rosemary sprigs and coarse sea salt. Bake in a preheated oven, 200°C/400°F/Gas Mark 6, for 20–25 minutes, until golden. Turn out to cool slightly. Serve warm.

pissaladière

easy   serves 6

1¾ hours   25–30 minutes

ingredients

100 ml/3½ fl oz hand-hot water
1 egg, beaten lightly
225 g/8 oz strong white bread flour,
    plus extra for dusting
1 tsp salt
25 g/1 oz butter, softened or diced
1 tsp easy-blend dried yeast
olive oil, for greasing

TOPPING
3 tsp olive oil
500 g/1 lb 2 oz red onions, sliced thinly
2 garlic cloves, chopped finely
2 tsp caster sugar
1½ tbsp balsamic vinegar
salt and pepper
100 g/3½ oz canned anchovy fillets, drained
12 black olives
1 tsp dried marjoram

Pour the water into the bread pan and add the egg. Sprinkle the flour over the liquid to cover. Place the salt and butter in 2 corners of the pan. Indent the flour without exposing the liquid and add the yeast. Set the bread machine to the pizza dough or dough setting and press start. Remove the dough from the pan.

For the topping, heat the oil. Add the onions and garlic. Cook over a low heat for 30 minutes. Add the sugar, vinegar and seasoning. Cook, stirring for 5 minutes, then set aside to cool.

Knock back the dough gently on a lightly floured surface, then roll out into a 30 x 23-cm/12 x 9-inch rectangle. Place in a Swiss roll tin. Spread the onion mixture over the base of the dough. Arrange the anchovy fillets on top with the olives. Sprinkle with marjoram. Cover with oiled clingfilm and set aside in a warm place for 10–15 minutes. Remove the clingfilm and bake in a preheated oven, 200°C/400°F/Gas Mark 6, for 25–30 minutes.

These delightful specialities are absurdly easy to make using a bread machine, which produces results to rival a professional pâtissier. Bake simple sweet breads in the machine or push the boat out and make an elegant, twisted loaf of Cornish Saffron Bread. The bread machine is perfect for cake-making, too. Use it to mix yeast doughs to perfection before cooking in a mould or tin or shaping into buns. Give yourself a mid-morning pick-me-up, take a well-deserved break with afternoon tea or simply indulge your sweet tooth at any time of day.

coffee break &
teatime treats

malted fruit loaf

extremely easy

1 medium loaf

10 minutes

about 3 hours

ingredients

225 ml/7½ fl oz hand-hot water
2 tsp sunflower oil
2 tbsp malt extract
1½ tbsp treacle

350 g/12 oz plain flour
1 tsp salt
1 tsp easy-blend dried yeast
140 g/5 oz sultanas

Pour the water into the bread pan and add the sunflower oil, malt extract and treacle.

Sprinkle the flour over the liquid to cover. Place the salt in 1 corner of the pan. Indent the flour without exposing the liquid and add the yeast.

Set the bread machine to basic setting, medium crust. Five minutes before the end of kneading, add the sultanas.

When the cycle has finished, turn out the bread to cool.

cornish saffron bread

easy   1 loaf

2¾ hours   30–35
minutes

1 tsp saffron threads
200 ml/7 fl oz milk
2 eggs, beaten lightly
500 g/1 lb 2 oz strong white bread flour,
    plus extra for dusting
½ tsp salt
4 tbsp caster sugar

55 g/2 oz butter, melted
1 tsp easy-blend dried yeast
sunflower oil, for greasing

GLAZE
1–2 tbsp clear honey

Place the saffron threads in a small bowl. Heat 5 tablespoons of the milk in a small saucepan, pour it over the saffron and set aside for at least 30 minutes. Pour the saffron milk and remaining milk into the bread pan and add the eggs. Sprinkle the flour over the liquid to cover. Place the salt, sugar and butter in 3 corners of the pan. Indent the flour without exposing the liquid and add the yeast. Set the bread machine to the dough setting and press start.

Remove the finished dough from the pan. Knock back gently on a floured surface, then divide it into 2 long ropes and twist together. Place on a greased baking sheet, cover with oiled clingfilm and set aside in a warm place for about 1 hour to rise. Heat the honey for the glaze in a small pan until runny. Remove the clingfilm and brush over the loaf. Bake in a preheated oven, 190°C/375°F/ Gas Mark 5, for 20 minutes. Lower to 180°C/350°F/Gas Mark 4 and bake for a further 10–15 minutes, until golden. Turn out to cool.

hungarian coffee cake

easy   1 loaf

2½ hours   55–60
minutes

ingredients

5 tbsp strong black coffee
2 tbsp brandy
1 cinnamon stick
115 g/4 oz raisins
2 tbsp hand-hot milk
3 eggs
500 g/1 lb 2 oz strong white
  bread flour

½ tsp salt
85 g/3 oz caster sugar
2 tsp easy-blend dried yeast
85 g/3 oz butter, melted, plus
  extra for greasing
sunflower oil, for greasing
2 egg whites
icing sugar, for dusting

Pour the coffee into a small pan. Add the brandy and cinnamon stick and heat. Add the raisins. Set aside for 30 minutes. Pour the milk into the bread pan and strain in the coffee mixture. Discard the cinnamon stick and reserve the raisins. Add the eggs. Sprinkle the flour over the liquid to cover. Add the salt and sugar. Indent the flour without exposing the liquid and add the yeast. Set the machine to the dough setting and press start. Add the butter in thirds at 5-minute intervals from the start.

Turn out the finished dough into a bowl. Knead in the reserved raisins. Grease a large brioche mould with butter. Whisk the egg whites to soft peaks. Gradually fold them into the dough. Spoon the dough into the brioche mould, cover with oiled clingfilm and set aside in a warm place for 1¼–1½ hours to rise. Remove the clingfilm and bake in a preheated oven, 190°C/375°F/Gas Mark 5, for 55–60 minutes. Cool, then dust with icing sugar before serving.

apple & walnut streusel cake

easy | one 25-cm/ 10-inch cake

2¼ hours | 30 minutes

ingredients

100 ml/3½ fl oz hand-hot milk
1 egg, beaten lightly
250 g/9 oz strong white bread flour,
  plus extra for dusting
½ tsp salt
3 tbsp caster sugar
25 g/1 oz butter, melted
1 tsp easy-blend dried yeast
sunflower oil, for greasing

TOPPING
115 g/4 oz plain flour
55 g/2 oz butter, diced
55 g/2 oz walnuts, chopped finely
4 tbsp caster sugar
1 tsp ground cinnamon
4 eating apples
2 tbsp lemon juice

Pour the milk into the bread pan and add the egg. Sprinkle the flour over the liquid to cover. Add the salt, sugar and butter. Indent the flour without exposing the liquid and add the yeast. Set the bread machine to the dough setting and press start. For the topping, sift the flour into a bowl and add the butter. Rub in. Stir in the walnuts, sugar and cinnamon. Set aside.

Lightly grease a 25-cm/10-inch springform cake tin. Remove the finished dough from the pan. Knock back gently on a floured surface, then roll out to fit the tin. Peel, core and thinly slice the apples. Toss them in the lemon juice and arrange on top of the dough. Sprinkle the nut topping over them. Cover the cake with lightly oiled clingfilm and set aside in a warm place for 25–30 minutes to rise. Remove the clingfilm and bake the cake in a preheated oven, 190°C/375°F/Gas Mark 5, for about 30 minutes, until golden. Leave in the tin to cool for 5 minutes, then turn out.

sticky apricot & cinnamon buns

easy · 12 buns

2½ hours · 20 minutes

ingredients

225 ml/7½ fl oz hand-hot milk
1 egg, beaten lightly
500 g/1 lb 2 oz strong white bread flour,
    plus extra for dusting
½ tsp salt
85 g/3 oz caster sugar
55 g/2 oz butter, softened or diced
1 tsp easy-blend dried yeast
sunflower oil, for greasing

FILLING
25 g/1 oz butter, melted
115 g/4 oz ready-to-eat dried
    apricots, chopped
55 g/2 oz sultanas
2 tbsp light brown sugar
1½ tsp ground cinnamon

GLAZE
4 tbsp water
4 tbsp caster sugar
1 tsp Amaretto liqueur

Pour the milk into the bread pan and add the egg. Sprinkle the flour over the liquid to cover. Add the salt, sugar and butter. Indent the flour without exposing the liquid and add the yeast. Set the machine to the dough setting and press start. Remove the finished dough from the pan. Knock back on a floured surface. Roll out into a 30-cm/12-inch square. For the filling, brush the dough with the butter, then sprinkle over the apricots, sultanas, sugar and cinnamon, leaving a border on one edge. Roll up towards the border, and seal. Cut into 12 slices. Place in a 23-cm/9-inch cake tin, with the cut sides upwards. Cover with clingfilm and set aside in a warm place for about 45 minutes to rise. Remove the clingfilm and bake in a preheated oven, 200°C/400°F/Gas Mark 6, for about 20 minutes. Cool for 5 minutes, then turn out.

For the glaze bring the water and sugar to the boil in a small pan, stirring constantly. Boil for 1½–2 minutes, not stirring, until syrupy. Stir in the liqueur and brush over the buns. Serve warm or cold.

devonshire splits

easy   8 buns

3 hours   15 minutes

ingredients

150 ml/5 fl oz hand-hot milk
225 g/8 oz strong white bread flour,
    plus extra for dusting
½ tsp salt
2 tbsp caster sugar
1 tsp easy-blend dried yeast
sunflower oil, for greasing
icing sugar, for dusting

FILLING
strawberry jam
double cream, whipped stiffly,
    or clotted cream

Pour the milk into the pan. Sprinkle the flour over the liquid to cover. Place the salt and sugar in 2 corners of the pan. Indent the flour without exposing the liquid and add the yeast. Set the bread machine to the dough setting and press start.

Remove the finished dough from the pan. Knock back gently on a lightly floured surface. Divide into 8 equal pieces and shape each one into a ball. Place on 2 lightly greased baking sheets and flatten the tops slightly. Cover with lightly oiled clingfilm and set aside in a warm place for about 45 minutes to rise.

Remove the clingfilm and bake in a preheated oven, 220°C/425°F/ Gas Mark 7, for about 15 minutes, until golden. Turn out to cool completely.

When the buns are cold, cut them open and fill with strawberry jam and cream. Dust with icing sugar and serve.

index